CHAPTER 1: THE ENTREPRENEURIAL JOURNEY

Introduction: Embracing the Path of Entrepreneurship

Embarking on the path of entrepreneurship is a transformative decision, but it's not reserved for a select few. The question is not whether anyone can become an entrepreneur, but rather if they are willing to embrace the challenges that lie ahead. This chapter sets the stage for your entrepreneurial odyssey by exploring the key attributes and skills necessary to thrive in this dynamic realm.

Cultivating Entrepreneurial Traits

- Developing the essential skills and characteristics: Discover the core traits of successful entrepreneurs, including creativity, adaptability, resilience, and visionary thinking. Understand how these qualities play a vital role in shaping your entrepreneurial journey.
- Learning through failure: Embrace the idea that failure is not a dead end but a stepping stone towards success. Explore how failures and setbacks can be valuable opportunities for learning and growth.

The Dream, Vision, and Future

- Crafting a sustainable dream: Learn to envision your business idea through the lens of the future. Explore the importance of creating a business concept that remains relevant and viable even in a rapidly evolving landscape.
- Identifying problems and innovative solutions: Understand the significance of addressing real-world problems through innovative solutions. Explore methodologies for brainstorming and ideation to create business ideas that stand the test of time.

Overcoming Entrepreneurial Challenges

- Navigating the funding landscape: Delve into the challenges of securing funding for your startup and explore strategies like bootstrapping and attracting investors.
- Standing out in a competitive market: Recognize the importance of differentiation and uniqueness in the face of competition. Learn how to communicate your unique selling proposition effectively to your target audience.
- Time management and prioritization: Discover effective ways to manage time and tasks efficiently, optimizing your focus on essential aspects of business growth.
- Strategic risk-taking: Understand the balance between taking risks and ensuring thoughtful decision-making. Explore the significance of market research, prototyping, and customer feedback in managing risk.

Sustaining Entrepreneurial Spirit

- Cultivating creativity and innovation: Explore methods to foster creativity and innovation within yourself and your business, ensuring continuous growth and progress.

- Leveraging technology for success: Recognize the transformative impact of technology on entrepreneurship. Learn how to utilize digital tools to expand your reach, automate processes, and make data-driven decisions.
- The art of evangelism: Master the art of promoting and advocating for your business, building a loyal customer base, and establishing your brand's authority in the industry.

Embracing Speed and Strength

- The power of agility: Understand the significance of acting quickly and decisively in the fast-paced world of entrepreneurship. Learn how speed can be a strategic advantage for staying ahead of the competition and seizing opportunities.
- Building resilience and stamina: Cultivate mental and emotional strength to endure the challenges and uncertainties that accompany the entrepreneurial journey.

This chapter lays the foundation for your entrepreneurial aspirations, guiding you through the essential qualities, strategic approaches, and challenges that await on this transformative path.

CHAPTER 2: IGNITING THE SPARK

Entrepreneurship is a thrilling journey filled with challenges and opportunities. At its core, lies the art of generating innovative ideas that can pave the way to success. Whether you're crafting a novel product, revolutionizing a service, or seeking ways to elevate an existing offering, the ability to nurture a constant flow of creative concepts is key to standing out in a bustling marketplace. In this chapter, we delve into the strategies that can ignite the entrepreneurial spark of creativity and explore real-life instances of successful businesses that harnessed these approaches to foster innovation.

Capturing Brilliance: The Idea Board and Notebook Method

Harnessing the power of simplicity, one of the most effective strategies for cultivating innovation is maintaining an idea board or a trusty notebook. These tools serve as a canvas to jot down every spark of inspiration. Regularly revisiting these notes helps identify patterns and themes that can be nurtured into groundbreaking ideas.

Example: Google Google's legendary co-founders, Larry Page and Sergey Brin, believed in the magic of their personal notebooks, where they documented ideas and daring experiments. The fruits of their dedication birthed the groundbreaking PageRank algorithm, the very core of Google's renowned search engine. Even today, Google continues to foster innovation, encouraging its employees to dedicate "20% time" to explore their own ideas, leading to the birth of transformative products like Google Maps and Gmail.

Crossing Boundaries: Seeking Inspiration from Diverse Industries

Innovation often blossoms by venturing beyond the confines of one's industry. Drawing inspiration from thriving businesses in other domains opens new vistas of ideas and methodologies that can be adapted and integrated into your own entrepreneurial ventures.

Example: Zappos Zappos, the celebrated online shoe and clothing retailer, owes its triumph to a customer-focused ethos inspired by the hospitality industry. Founder Tony Hsieh envisioned a corporate culture that prioritized customer service and employee happiness. This visionary outlook led Zappos to become one of the most successful online retailers worldwide.

Collaborative Brilliance: Brainstorming with a Cohesive Team

Unleashing the collective creativity of a cohesive team through brainstorming sessions can generate a dynamic environment that fuels innovation. When each team member contributes ideas and builds upon each other's concepts, groundbreaking solutions can emerge.

Example: IDEO IDEA, the global design powerhouse, champions the "design thinking" approach, laying emphasis on collaboration and brainstorming. Their teams engage in idea generation and create prototypes that undergo real-world testing to ensure they meet user needs, leading to innovative and user-centric products and experiences.

Unearthing Opportunities: Conducting Thorough Market Research

Market research is an indispensable tool to understand customer needs and preferences. Identifying gaps in the market and potential areas for improvement can be the catalysts that propel your business towards innovation and differentiation.

Example: Airbnb Airbnb, the trailblazing home-sharing platform, conducted extensive market research to unearth the demand for unique and affordable accommodations in popular travel destinations. Focused on this niche, Airbnb disrupted the traditional travel industry and soared to the ranks of one of the most successful startups in history.

Unwinding for Brilliance: The Power of Taking Breaks

Sometimes, innovation flourishes when we least expect it. Taking breaks and engaging in activities that allow the mind to unwind can offer a fresh perspective and stimulate new waves of creative thinking.

Example: Pixar The animation genius, Pixar, encourages its employees to embark on "plaid days" - moments devoted to personal projects or simply relaxing away from work. These breaks serve as wellsprings of creativity, vital to the success of their awe-inspiring films.

Embracing Failure as the Stepping Stone

Embracing failure as a stepping stone to success is a hallmark of true innovators. Experimentation and taking calculated risks pave the way for refining ideas and achieving breakthroughs.

Example: Amazon Jeff Bezos, Amazon's visionary founder, famously acknowledges the inseparable bond between failure and invention. Amazon's culture fosters experimentation and innovation, even if it means facing short-term risks. This bold approach has led to transformative products like the Amazon Echo and the Amazon Prime subscription service.

Embracing the Tech Frontier: Leveraging Emerging Technologies

The ever-evolving tech frontier offers a treasure trove of opportunities for innovation. Embracing emerging technologies in your domain empowers you to stay ahead of the competition and redefine the boundaries of what's possible.

Example: Tesla Tesla, the trailblazing electric car company, harnesses emerging technologies such as artificial intelligence and self-driving capabilities to create high-performance electric vehicles. Their focus on technology has propelled Tesla to become a symbol of innovation and leadership in the automotive industry.

Collaborating for Success: Networking with Fellow Entrepreneurs

Collaborating with fellow entrepreneurs and experts in your field fosters a rich exchange of ideas and diverse perspectives.

Example: Kickstarter The renowned crowdfunding platform, Kickstarter, emerged from the joint vision of a team of enterprising individuals seeking to empower artists and creators. Today, it has blossomed into a hub of collaboration and innovation, where creators can showcase their ideas and seek support from an enthusiastic community.

Riding the Waves of Change: Staying Informed about Industry Trends

Keeping a finger on the pulse of industry trends reveals new avenues for innovation. Staying informed and adaptable to emerging trends enables you to seize opportunities and evolve your business strategy.

Example: Netflix Netflix, the trailblazing streaming media company, preserves its leadership by continuously adapting to industry trends. Embracing novel forms of content, such as original programming and interactive storytelling, keeps Netflix at the forefront of an ever-changing media landscape.

In conclusion, cultivating creativity and unleashing the entrepreneurial spirit of innovation are vital for the success of any entrepreneur. By adopting strategies such as these, you can nurture a steady stream of groundbreaking ideas that set your business apart in a competitive marketplace. Remember, there's no one-size-fits-all approach to generating ideas, so experimentation with different strategies is key to discovering what works best for you and your business.

CHAPTER 3: THE ALCHEMY OF INNOVATION: UNEARTHING BILLION-DOLLAR IDEATION

In the vast landscape of entrepreneurship, the pursuit of a billion-dollar idea can appear like an elusive treasure. However, history has proven that remarkable innovators have navigated this path before. Here, we embark on a transformative journey to unlock the secrets of generating billion-dollar ideas.

Illuminating the Vision: Igniting Creativity

To set the wheels in motion, one must ignite creativity's flame. Embrace the power of ideation by seeking inspiration from diverse sources and allowing the mind to wander freely. Step outside the confines of conventional thinking and explore uncharted territories. Unravel problems that call for ingenious solutions, as they often hold the key to extraordinary success.

Example: The Miraculous Marker A simple yet profound idea led to the invention of the dry erase marker. In the 1950s, Jerry Woolf experimented with a marker that used a combination of ink and a film that could be wiped clean with a cloth. This innovation birthed the modern-day whiteboard and revolutionized communication and learning worldwide.

Embracing Techno-savvy: Riding the Waves of Technology

The realm of technology offers a treasure trove of possibilities. Stay attuned to emerging trends and technological advancements. Consider how new breakthroughs can converge with existing industries to create groundbreaking products or services. By embracing the wave of innovation, you can ride towards an unparalleled opportunity.

Example: Cryptocurrency Chronicles Satoshi Nakamoto's ingenious concept of Bitcoin amalgamated cryptography and decentralized technology to create the world's first cryptocurrency. This trailblazing idea paved the way for a revolutionary digital economy and transformed the financial landscape.

Empathy Unleashed: Understanding Real Needs

In the pursuit of billion-dollar ideas, genuine empathy becomes an invaluable ally. Observe and understand the needs and pain points of the people around you. Seek out opportunities to make a positive impact on their lives by addressing unmet desires or challenges. Transforming empathy into action can lead to awe-inspiring innovations.

Example: The Guardian of Sight Dr. Sanduk Ruit, an ophthalmologist from Nepal, recognized the plight of individuals suffering from cataracts in remote areas. He co-founded the Himalayan Cataract Project, pioneering an innovative and cost-effective cataract surgery technique. This compassionate endeavor has restored sight to countless people, transforming lives across the Himalayas and beyond.

Niche Adventures: Exploring Uncharted Markets

Often hidden within niches lie untapped potential for billion-dollar ideas. Identify underrepresented markets with specific demands, and tailor offerings to meet their unique requirements. Focused ventures can create significant ripples, disrupting industries and carving out extraordinary success.

Example: Beyond the Bean Starbucks, with its unique approach to coffeehouses, ventured beyond the standard coffee experience. By creating a cozy environment and offering premium coffee, they unlocked a niche market and sparked a global coffee culture phenomenon.

Rethinking the Classics: Innovating on Tradition

Grand ideas can emerge from reimagining and reinventing classics. Examine established products or services and discover opportunities for enhancement or evolution. Adding a novel twist or combining existing elements can create captivating propositions with transformative potential.

Example: Virtual Reality Renaissance Oculus, led by Palmer Luckey, reinvigorated virtual reality by developing Oculus Rift. The innovative combination of cutting-edge technology and immersive experiences unlocked new dimensions of entertainment, gaming, and beyond.

Scaling the Heights: Pioneering Massive Goals

To reach billion-dollar heights, dare to dream big and set ambitious goals. Though the journey may start small, with perseverance and an unwavering vision, exponential growth becomes attainable. A foundation built on grand aspirations provides the springboard for success.

Example: SpaceX's Cosmic Ambitions Elon Musk's SpaceX commenced as a venture to make space travel more accessible and affordable. With ambitious goals and groundbreaking innovations, the company transformed the space industry, pioneering reusable rockets and interplanetary aspirations.

Innovation thrives in the realm of collaborative brilliance. Unite with like-minded individuals, each contributing unique expertise and perspectives. Foster a culture of innovation, where ideas fuse and multiply, transcending individual capabilities to achieve monumental impact.

In conclusion, the path to a billion-dollar idea lies in the nexus of creativity, technology, empathy, niche exploration, reimagining classics, pursuing ambitious goals, and dynamic collaboration. By embarking on this transformative journey, we unlock the alchemy of innovation that has the potential to reshape industries and touch lives on a global scale.

CHAPTER 4: THE ENTREPRENEUR'S QUEST: DECODING CHALLENGES THROUGH INGENIOUS SOLUTIONS

In the realm of entrepreneurship, navigating challenges and devising innovative solutions is the ultimate adventure. This chapter explores the pivotal role of problem-solving in the entrepreneurial journey and unveils effective strategies for identifying problems and crafting transformative answers, accompanied by inspirational tales of entrepreneurial brilliance.

Section 1: The Heartbeat of Entrepreneurship: Embracing Problem-Solving

At the core of entrepreneurship lies problem-solving, the lifeblood that sustains and propels visionary individuals forward. Embracing this dynamic process involves an array of steps, each leading entrepreneurs closer to success in their quests for change.

Section 2: Illuminating the Path: Understanding the Essence of the Problem

To conquer any challenge, a profound understanding of its essence is indispensable. Entrepreneurs embark on research expeditions, unraveling the root causes, implications, and potential solutions. Empowered by knowledge, they equip themselves with the wisdom to carve their paths ahead.

Section 3: Navigating Uncharted Territories: The Power of Market Insight

As the problem comes into focus, the market beckons with its enigmatic allure. Entrepreneurial visionaries harness the power of market insight, navigating uncharted territories to gauge the demand for their solutions and chart a course towards success.

Section 4: Igniting the Spark: The Renaissance of Ideas

In the crucible of creativity, the spark of innovation ignites. Entrepreneurs embark on a visionary journey, igniting their imaginations and delving into the depths of limitless ideas. Unfettered by constraints, they forge groundbreaking solutions from the crucible of their minds.

Section 5: Forging the Masterpiece: Identifying the Optimal Solution

Amid the constellation of ideas, the optimal solution emerges as a masterpiece. Methodically evaluating potential answers against market demands and resources, entrepreneurs choose the path with the potential to bring about the most transformative impact.

Section 6: Crafting the Blueprint: A Comprehensive Plan Takes Shape

With the optimal solution in hand, entrepreneurs craft a comprehensive blueprint, illuminating the path to realization. In this carefully architected plan, objectives stand tall, strategies intertwine, tactics emerge, timelines beckon, and resources fall into place.

Section 7: Bridging Imagination and Reality: Building a Prototype

Before dreams take flight, they must find form. Entrepreneurs breathe life into their visions by building prototypes, tangible representations of their solutions. Here, they test, refine, and fine-tune their creations, seeking perfection before the grand unveiling.

Section 8: Unveiling the Vision: Gathering Feedback

With prototypes in hand, the curtains rise, and entrepreneurs eagerly seek feedback from their audience and stakeholders. Engaging in a dialogue of discovery, they use the insights gained to bring their visions to even greater heights.

Section 9: The Entrepreneurial Symphony: Launching the Solution

The time for action has arrived. Entrepreneurs stand center stage as they launch their solutions into the world. A symphony of marketing and sales strategies fill the air, heralding the arrival of transformative change.

Section 10: The Dance of Evolution: Embracing Continuous Improvement

In the realm of entrepreneurship, evolution is perpetual. Entrepreneurs dance with change, continually gathering feedback, monitoring performance, and adapting to the dynamic currents of the market. A tireless quest for perfection propels them forward in their never-ending odyssey.

Example 1: Empowering Education through Technology

Sarah's vision soared beyond horizons as she recognized the educational disparity in remote areas. Armed with technology and compassion, she founded an ed-tech platform that empowered students with access to quality education. Her innovative solution bridged the gap, transforming lives and illuminating the way towards a brighter future.

Example 2: Sparking Green Revolution: Sustainable Agriculture

Jason's heart was bound to the soil, and his mind fixated on preserving the planet. Fuelled by a passion for sustainable agriculture, he launched a startup that developed cutting-edge farming techniques. These revolutionary methods nurtured crops while preserving nature, pioneering the green revolution.

CHAPTER 5: THE STRATEGIC FRAMEWORK FOR BUSINESS SUCCESS

Unleashing the Potential: The Business Model Canvas in Action

In the world of entrepreneurship, the Business Model Canvas emerges as a dynamic and strategic framework, unlocking the potential for business success. A comprehensive tool that delves into critical components, including customer segments, value propositions, channels, customer relationships, revenue streams, key activities, key resources, key partnerships, and cost structure, this canvas serves as a compass for entrepreneurs navigating the challenging waters of the market.

Understanding the Customer Landscape: The foundation of a thriving business lies in understanding the intricacies of the target customer segment. Demographics, psychographics, and behavior play pivotal roles in tailoring products and services to meet their unique needs and desires, creating a loyal and engaged customer base.

Crafting Compelling Value Propositions: In a crowded marketplace, a compelling value proposition becomes the beacon that draws customers in. By identifying key differentiators, be it cost-effectiveness, quality, or innovation, entrepreneurs can clearly communicate the unmatched value their offerings bring to the table.

Navigating Channels for Success: Mastering the art of reaching and engaging customers demands a strategic approach to channels. Digital platforms, social media, brick-and-mortar establishments, and other avenues converge to provide a seamless and personalized experience, cementing the brand's presence in the market.

Building Lasting Customer Relationships: Customer relationships are the backbone of a sustainable business.

By delivering top-notch customer service, personalized experiences, and loyalty programs, businesses can nurture long-term connections, fostering brand advocacy and repeat business.

Diversifying Revenue Streams: In the quest for financial stability, the revenue streams component plays a pivotal role. Diversification of income sources, incorporating product sales, subscription models, partnerships, and more, empowers businesses to weather market fluctuations and drive growth.

Executing Key Activities with Precision: The engine driving value creation consists of key activities that demand precision and focus. From product development and marketing to customer support, seamless execution of these critical tasks sets the stage for success.

Leveraging Key Resources for Competitive Edge: Success in the market hinges on the strategic utilization of key resources. Physical assets, intellectual property, and human capital combine to form a potent arsenal that sets businesses apart and drives innovation.

Forging Strategic Key Partnerships: Thriving businesses understand the power of strategic partnerships. Collaborations with suppliers, distributors, and complementary ventures not only enhance efficiency but also unlock new avenues for growth and expansion.

Optimizing the Cost Structure: Financial prudence is a cornerstone of business resilience. A clear understanding of cost structures, both fixed and variable, empowers entrepreneurs to optimize spending while maximizing value delivery.

Conclusion: In the ever-evolving landscape of business, the Business Model Canvas remains a steadfast ally for entrepreneurs.

By meticulously mapping out the core components and their interconnections, businesses gain a competitive advantage and a profound understanding of their strategic positioning.
This iterative and adaptable framework fosters an environment of continuous improvement, enabling enterprises to stay ahead of the curve and meet the changing demands of the market.
Armed with the Business Model Canvas, entrepreneurs set sail on a journey towards sustainable growth, innovation, and lasting success.

CHAPTER 6: THE EMPIRICAL ODYSSEY: UNRAVELING AND PERFECTING YOUR BUSINESS CONCEPTS

Embarking on the journey of transforming your visionary ideas into a flourishing business demands an essential phase – the empirical odyssey.

In this chapter, we plunge into the realm of empirical assessment, unveiling an array of innovative methodologies to validate and refine your concepts. The process embraces the power of personal interviews, the prowess of data-driven insights, and a fresh perspective that sets the stage for entrepreneurial triumph.

The Illuminating Essence of Personal Interviews: Stepping into the world of successful business endeavors, personal interviews become the guiding light. They are the compass that navigates entrepreneurs towards understanding their audience and crafting products and services that truly resonate. While the idea of conducting interviews may evoke trepidation, recognizing their potential to create an indelible impact is what sets trailblazers apart. Interviews serve as the conduit to gather feedback, identify potential customers, and shape the very essence of your business model.

Empathy in B2C Engagement: The path to meaningful engagement with B2C customers begins by stepping out into the world, immersing oneself in the bustling streets of the target market. For startups catering to B2B, the journey involves delving into the corporate domain. Let's delve into an intriguing scenario, picturing a revolutionary mobile app named "SensioFolio," designed to capture emotions through artful photography. Armed with a well-crafted questionnaire, entrepreneurs, introducing themselves as the visionary creators of SensioFolio, venture forth to unlock the hearts and minds of potential interviewees.

During the interview process, the alchemy lies in fostering conversations, not merely executing a survey.

The seeds of success are sown through objectivity, refraining from offering excessive information that might skew responses. Begin with fundamental queries like names, ages, and occupations to delineate the customer segment. Gradually, unfurl open-ended questions such as "How do you connect with art and emotions?" or "What role does photography play in expressing your feelings?"

Unraveling the mysteries of emotions and artistry illuminates valuable insights into the desires and pain points of the target audience.

Avoiding the Quicksand of Common Interview Mistakes: Guidance through the empirical odyssey necessitates sidestepping common pitfalls that lurk in the interview process. One such quagmire is the "which" question without follow-up, leading to fleeting responses that withhold genuine depth. Liberating the interviews from the shackles of surveys, for authenticity is compromised in written responses. Vital interactions flourish when conducted face-to-face, transcending the boundaries of telephonic conversations. Lastly, the endeavor demands detachment from the comfort of friends and family, embracing the raw honesty only strangers can impart.

Unveiling the Tapestry of Insights: With interviews conducted, the treasure trove of insights demands preservation and analysis. Recordings become the archives of wisdom, while aiming for a bounty of a hundred interviews nurtures robust conclusions. The endeavor entails connecting with at least twenty customers weekly over five weeks to fine-tune the questionnaire and canvas. These enriching interviews weave together the threads of customer segments, value propositions, and the canvas of the business model. A fellow voyager joining this odyssey as a confidante, to both observe and transcribe the conversations, elevates the collective understanding.

Empowering the B2B Odyssey: For founders embarking on the B2B odyssey, comprehending the essence of their target customers becomes paramount. The guiding star is conducting interviews with B2B enterprises, unlocking the secrets to their needs and aspirations.

The quest may seem daunting, but every stride in this direction is a stride towards success.

Sailing the Seas of B2B Interaction: The voyage into the realm of B2B interviews requires meticulous preparation and finesse. Immersing oneself in extensive research about the industry and the specific business is the cornerstone. A personalized approach, introducing oneself as a seeker of market wisdom, earns the privilege of conducting interviews with B2B enterprises. A carefully curated list of open-ended questions becomes the compass, illuminating the path to understanding the challenges, needs, and aspirations of these businesses. Through attentive listening and follow-up queries, entrepreneurs glean profound insights, steering the course towards addressing the unique demands of B2B customers.

A Symphony of Insights - An Entrepreneurial Overture: Imagine a start-up revolutionizing the hospitality industry with AI-powered concierge services. Picture the orchestrator of this entrepreneurial symphony conducting interviews with upscale hotels. The notes of inquiry resonate, seeking to understand how personalization and convenience intertwine in the world of luxury hospitality. The crescendo of conversations yields invaluable insights that inform the very architecture of this revolutionary enterprise.

In Conclusion: The Empirical Odyssey and Entrepreneurial Triumph The empirical odyssey stands as a crucial rite of passage for entrepreneurial triumph. Through the alchemy of personal interviews and the magic of data-driven insights, entrepreneurs unravel the tapestry of their target audience's desires, refining their concepts to resonate deeply with their clientele. With every step of this journey, the entrepreneur embraces the spirit of flexibility, knowing that their vision might transform and flourish through the wisdom of feedback. Empowered by the empirical odyssey, entrepreneurs unveil their ventures to the world, embarking on a grand entrepreneurial overture that captivates hearts and disrupts industries.

CHAPTER 7: INNOVATING BEYOND THE MINIMUM VIABLE PRODUCT

In today's fast-paced and competitive market, creating a Minimum Viable Product (MVP) is no longer enough to ensure success. While the concept of an MVP has been a game-changer, it's time to explore new perspectives and strategies to take your product development to the next level. In this chapter, we will delve into innovative approaches that go beyond the traditional MVP, enabling you to captivate your audience, gather invaluable feedback, and boost your chances of long-term success.

The "Concierge Enigma": Elevating the MVP Experience

Imagine this: a personalized, high-touch service delivered to a select group of early adopters. Welcome to the "Concierge Enigma," a novel approach to MVP testing. Rather than offering a basic prototype, provide an exclusive and tailored experience to a small group of potential customers. This approach allows you to assess the viability of your software product concept while also nurturing a strong bond with early adopters.

For instance, let's say you are developing a personal shopping app. Instead of merely offering a digital platform, personally shop for customers and deliver their purchases to their doorstep. This hands-on experience not only tests the demand for your service but also creates a unique connection with your customers. Their feedback becomes invaluable, guiding you toward the perfect product-market fit.

The "Living Mockup": Breathing Life into Product Design

While traditional mockups are static representations of your product's interface, let's breathe life into them and create a "Living Mockup." Instead of presenting users with a rigid, non-interactive design, provide them with a dynamic and clickable prototype. Utilize cutting-edge design tools that offer real-time interactions, enabling users to explore your product's interface and provide instantaneous feedback.

For example, when developing a new mobile app for tracking daily water intake, utilize design tools like Figma or InVision to create a living mockup. This clickable prototype allows users to interact with the app, add water intake, and explore various features. The feedback garnered from this immersive experience becomes invaluable, steering your product toward optimal usability and visual appeal.

The "Wizard's Rehearsal": Preparing for Automated Success

Automation has become a defining aspect of modern software products. Enter the "Wizard's Rehearsal," a unique take on the MVP for automation-driven products. Rather than investing in complex programming upfront, manually perform the functions your software aims to automate. This approach allows you to validate the usefulness and engagement of your product concept before diving into full development.

Consider developing a chatbot or voice assistant for booking restaurant reservations or travel. Instead of automated responses, have a team member personally handle users' requests in real-time. This not only tests the concept but also provides valuable insights into user preferences and pain points, shaping the foundation for a successful automated product.

"Haptic MVP": Blending the Physical and Digital Worlds

In today's tech-driven world, it's easy to forget the significance of the physical experience. With the "Haptic MVP," we merge the physical and digital realms to create a product that appeals to both senses and sensibilities. This approach is particularly relevant for hardware MVPs, where the tactile experience plays a crucial role.

For instance, when developing a smart home device or wearable, combine 3D printing and CNC machining to create a physical prototype. Allow potential users to interact with the device, touching and feeling its tangible features. The haptic feedback they provide will be invaluable in refining your product's design, functionality, and overall appeal.

In conclusion, the traditional MVP has opened doors for innovation, but it's time to take the next leap. Embrace the "Concierge Enigma" to build strong relationships with early adopters, adopt the "Living Mockup" to make your designs come alive, employ the "Wizard's Rehearsal" for automated success, and explore the "Haptic MVP" to bridge the physical and digital realms. By embracing these new perspectives, you'll be well on your way to creating a truly captivating and successful product that stands out in today's dynamic market.

CHAPTER 8: BUSINESS VELOCITY

In the ever-evolving landscape of business, the momentum gained by a company is what sets it apart from the rest - it's called "traction." Picture a roaring locomotive, relentless and unstoppable, as it acquires more customers, expands its reach, and generates greater revenue. Traction is the vital force that propels a business forward, signaling its health and potential. In this chapter, we'll delve into the captivating world of traction, exploring how to generate it and the diverse methods that unlock growth on an exponential scale.

Understanding Traction: The Pulse of a Thriving Business

Traction - a word whispered with reverence among entrepreneurs - is the rate at which a business is growing or acquiring customers. It is the heartbeat that determines a company's success, measured by essential metrics such as monthly active users, customer acquisition costs, and customer lifetime value. Picture a novel e-commerce platform gaining traction, gauged by the number of customers making purchases, the average order value, and the rate of repeat purchases. This pulse of momentum is the lifeblood of business success.

Mastering the Art of Generating Traction: A Symphony of Strategies

Generating traction requires a symphony of strategies orchestrated to resonate with your business and target audience. Among the virtuoso techniques lies growth hacking - a repertoire of experimentation and data-driven insights, leading to rapid and robust growth. A skilled conductor might employ A/B testing, referral marketing, and optimized app store listings to compose a crescendo of downloads for a new app.

Then there's social media marketing, the conductor's baton gracefully dancing across platforms to reach and engage the audience in a personal and captivating melody. Visual storytelling, influencer collaborations, and interactive engagements enthrall audiences, building a harmonious bond between the brand and its followers.

Viral marketing, like a contagious rhythm, spreads through word of mouth and social media shares. A well-crafted referral program and shareable, buzzworthy content create a chorus of excitement and brand evangelism.

Amidst this musical symphony, search engine optimization (SEO) takes center stage. The maestro fine-tunes website content to rank higher in search engine results. The result? A grand performance of visibility and increased traffic.

In the spotlight next is search engine marketing (SEM), a powerful soloist in generating traction. Paid advertising on search engines skillfully targets specific keywords, resonating with a highly engaged audience, amplifying the brand's message.

Let's not forget the magnetic power of word-of-mouth marketing, a virtuoso solo that captivates hearts and minds. Encouraging customers to share positive experiences like an impassioned encore, fueling growth through genuine advocacy.

Reaping the Fruits of Traction: Measuring Success

As the symphony of traction unfolds, the audience awaits the moment of triumph. Key metrics like monthly active users, customer acquisition costs, and customer lifetime value become the applause that measures success. The business conducts analytics, collecting insights from the audience to refine the performance.

In conclusion, the enchanting melody of traction is an essential component of building a thriving business.
By orchestrating growth hacking, social media marketing, viral marketing, search engine optimization, search engine marketing, and word-of-mouth marketing, businesses can command the stage, enrapture audiences, and achieve exponential expansion.
The conductor must stay nimble, allowing the audience's feedback to shape the symphony.
With each movement, the business evolves, thriving in the captivating symphony of success.

CHAPTER 9: UNLEASHING SYNERGY: CRAFTING AN EMPOWERED TEAM FOR BUSINESS SUCCESS

In the quest to build a thriving business, the true catalyst lies not only in a brilliant idea but in the cohesive force of a strong team. In this chapter, we embark on a journey to unravel the importance of assembling an empowered team, delving into the art of finding the ideal co-founder and developer, mastering the intricate dance of collaboration with friends, and embracing the pivotal role of discipline in molding a successful team.

The Dynamic Force of an Empowered Team: The Heartbeat of Success

A successful business is a symphony of talents, expertise, and experiences coming together in harmony - the essence of a well-constructed team. Assembling a powerhouse team unlocks the key to overcoming challenges, making informed decisions, and executing your vision with precision. Picture a new e-commerce platform taking shape, with a co-founder's business acumen, a developer's technical finesse, and a marketing specialist's digital prowess driving it forward. This united front of diverse skills and camaraderie weaves the fabric of your triumph.

Seeking the Perfect Co-founder: An Invaluable Partnership

Finding the perfect co-founder is akin to finding a kindred spirit. Together, you must share a vision, align values, and complement each other's strengths. Trust and effective collaboration are the foundation of this invaluable partnership. The roadmap to finding your co-founder follows these steps:

Step 1: Soul-search your strengths and weaknesses. Step 2: Seek a co-founder with complementary skills and experiences. Step 3: Engage in networking events and meetups to cross paths with potential co-founders.

Step 4: Leverage the vast resources of LinkedIn, AngelList, or co-founder matching platforms. Step 5: Nurture a meaningful relationship before solidifying the partnership.

For a tech startup, the ideal co-founder might exude technical prowess and boast a passion for the industry, harmoniously resonating with your vision.

Finding the Coding Virtuoso: A Technical Masterpiece

In the realm of tech business, a skilled developer is the architect who breathes life into your product. Seek a developer with the requisite technical skills and experience, someone you can collaborate with effortlessly. The steps to finding this coding virtuoso are as follows:

Step 1: Define the technical skills and experience your project demands. Step 2: Pursue developers experienced in your industry or niche. Step 3: Engage with tech conferences and hackathons to cross paths with potential developers. Step 4: Harness the digital resources of GitHub, Stack Overflow, or Upwork to uncover exceptional talent. Step 5: Evaluate candidates' portfolios, resumes, and references meticulously before extending an offer.

For a mobile app venture, the ideal developer would wield a strong portfolio of successful projects, honed in the art of mobile app development.

The Balancing Act of Working with Friends: Nurturing Bonds and Boundaries

Working with friends brings both warmth and complexity. The trust and support they bring can be invaluable, but personal dynamics may occasionally blur the lines. To harmoniously navigate this journey, adhere to these tips:

Tip 1: Establish clear boundaries and expectations from the outset. Tip 2: Embrace open and honest communication with each other.

Tip 3: Dedicate time for personal and professional development. Tip 4: Confront conflicts directly and proactively. Tip 5: Celebrate shared achievements and milestones.

In the context of building a marketing agency with a friend, delineating roles and responsibilities, maintaining transparent communication, and fostering team-building endeavors are pivotal to success.

The Maestro of Discipline: Orchestrating Success

Discipline is the guiding baton that conducts a successful team. It involves defining clear objectives and expectations, instilling a culture of accountability and ownership, and upholding a consistent work ethic. With discipline as your melody, you remain focused, motivated, and productive, even in the face of adversity.

For a new software development team, establishing precise project timelines, employing project management tools for progress tracking, and conducting regular reviews ensure the team stays on course.

In conclusion, the nucleus of a triumphant business lies in a robust team. Whether seeking a co-founder, developer, or collaborating with friends, identifying the right blend of skills, experiences, and personalities is paramount. Nurturing discipline and accountability within your team will yield fruitful results, transforming your vision into reality. These strategies will equip you to cultivate an empowered team, fostering a harmonious journey toward success.

CHAPTER 10: WEAVING THE TAPESTRY OF SUCCESS: THE ART OF UNVEILING YOUR STARTUP'S MAGIC THROUGH STORYTELLING

In the wondrous world of startups, the journey to success lies not only in the brilliance of your idea but also in the art of enchanting your audience through the spellbinding act of pitching. Picture yourself on a grand stage, where you become a master storyteller, effortlessly weaving a tapestry of captivating tales that breathe life into your business vision, enthralling investors, customers, and partners alike. In this chapter, we embark on a transformative quest to explore the power of storytelling, the alchemy of crafting compelling pitch decks, the charm of an elevator pitch, and the magic that lies within the enigmatic act of pitching your business.

The Spellbinding Symphony of Pitching: Unveiling the Magic of Storytelling

Pitching, the grand orchestration of presenting your business idea, product, or service to potential investors, customers, or partners, holds the key to unlocking the doors of success. Just as a symphony resonates through the hearts of its listeners, your pitch must resonate with your audience, conjuring a connection that tugs at their emotions and ignites their curiosity.

Envision, for instance, the unveiling of a new e-commerce platform. In the spotlight, you become the conductor, leading your audience on a journey through the market's wonders, the platform's enchanting features, and the spellbinding projections of future growth.

The Kaleidoscope of Pitch Decks: Crafting Harmonious Presentations to Captivate

Within the realm of pitch decks, an array of kaleidoscopic possibilities awaits, each designed to cater to a specific audience and purpose. Let us explore these enchanting presentations:

Elevator Pitch - A brief yet mesmerizing performance, akin to a fleeting breeze that whisks you away on an adventure. In its concise moments, the elevator pitch encapsulates the very essence of your business idea, leaving your audience spellbound and yearning for more.

Imagine delivering an elevator pitch for a new mobile app, delicately weaving the tale of its transformative solution to a pressing problem, the alluring features that set it apart, and the enchanting market opportunity that beckons.

3-minute Investor Pitch - As the curtains rise, the 3-minute investor pitch takes center stage, offering a more intricate performance. Within its captivating span, it must eloquently communicate the vital elements of your business idea to potential investors - a crystal-clear problem statement, a resplendent solution, the alluring market opportunity, and your unique value proposition.

For instance, envision a 3-minute investor pitch for a new SaaS platform, adorning the stage with the tale of customers' pain points, the symphony of features that delight, the celestial promise of revenue streams, and the dance with competitors in the market.

15-minute Investor Pitch - The crescendo of enchantment reaches its zenith with the 15-minute investor pitch, unveiling a comprehensive panorama of your business idea. Within this captivating performance, you showcase the enigmatic puzzle pieces that make up your vision - the enlivening problem you seek to solve, the celestial market opportunity, the virtuosic team behind it all, the harmonious product or service, the alchemical revenue model, and the enchanting financial projections.

Envision, for instance, a 15-minute investor pitch for a new healthcare startup, enchanting the audience with the profound significance of the unique problem your solution addresses, the boundless potential of the market, the key features that inspire awe, and the resplendent tapestry of competitors.

The Enigmatic Allure of Storytelling: Elevating Your Pitch with Emotional Connection

Amidst the grand performance of pitching, the mystique of storytelling emerges as a potent elixir to forge emotional connections with your audience. Just as an enthralling fairy tale lingers in the hearts of its listeners, so too does a compelling narrative linger in the minds of investors, casting an enduring spell that separates your business from the rest.

Through storytelling, your pitch transcends the ordinary, weaving a magical aura around your business and instilling the audience with a deep sense of purpose and passion. In this symphony of enchantment, investors grasp the value of your business and its potential to bring about positive change in the world.

For instance, envision pitching a new eco-friendly cleaning product, where your storytelling prowess transports investors to a world fraught with environmental harm from traditional cleaning products. As they immerse themselves in your tale, they become enchanted with the possibilities of your eco-friendly alternative - reducing waste, fostering sustainability, and dancing in harmony with Mother Nature.

The Alchemy of Craftsmanship: Unveiling the Potent Elements of Your Narrative

Within the grand tapestry of storytelling, you possess a myriad of enchanting elements to infuse into your pitch:

Personal Story - As the founder of a new mental health app, you share a personal tale that inspired your noble quest. Imagine revealing your struggles with mental health and how existing solutions fell short in meeting your profound needs. This personal connection weaves an intimate bond with investors, allowing them to witness your genuine passion in solving a real problem.

Customer Story - Picture yourself pitching a new e-commerce platform, adorned with an alluring customer story that exemplifies the transformative benefits of your product or service. Imagine the mesmerizing testimonial of a satisfied customer, recounting their delight with your platform's ease of use, the abundance of products, and the blissful embrace of excellent customer service. This customer story kindles investors' imaginations, allowing them to envision the enchanting allure of your offering.

Vision Story - For a sustainable energy company, your pitch emanates a radiant vision story, painting the cosmic canvas of your long-term goals. Within this enchanting tale, you speak of a world where clean and renewable energy reigns supreme, and your technology serves as the catalyst for this harmonious transformation. This vision story kindles a grand vision within investors' hearts, inspiring them to become part of the magical journey.

Brand Story - Imagine pitching a new food delivery service, where a brand story of remarkable charm unfolds. Your tale weaves the very values and mission that propel your business - a commitment to locally sourced ingredients, the noble crusade against food waste, and the symphony of wholesome and delectable meals for your customers. This brand story imbues investors with a profound sense of the unique value your business brings to the table.

The Enigmatic Elevator Pitch: A Spellbinding Incantation

To captivate your audience with an unforgettable elevator pitch, you must master the alchemical art of crafting one that resonates deeply with its recipients:

> Focus on the profound problem you solve and the enchanting value you bestow.
> Employ simple and evocative language, conjuring images that dance within their minds.
> Keep your pitch delightfully concise, leaving them yearning for more.
> Weave enchanting examples or anecdotes into your narrative, sparking their curiosity and wonder.
> Practice your incantation until it flows effortlessly from your lips, exuding confidence and charm.

As the spotlight finds you, imagine uttering the following enchanting elevator pitch:

"Behold, I am [Name], the mastermind behind [Company Name], where magic and innovation intertwine. Our wondrous [Industry/Field] company is rewriting the rules of [Mission Statement], and our transformative [Product/Service] shines with an enchanting radiance. As I tread upon this enchanted path, I'm driven by the vision of creating a solution that can [Benefit], a vision that echoes in harmony with every heart we touch. Join us, and together we shall summon a future of endless possibilities and dazzling success. Are you prepared to embrace the magic?"

In conclusion, the art of pitching is a mesmerizing dance that merges creativity, passion, and persuasion. Through the magic of storytelling and the eloquence of your pitch, you can unveil the soul of your startup, capturing the hearts and minds of your audience. Embrace the enchantment of pitching, and let your startup's magic shine brightly in the world of possibilities.

CHAPTER 11: THE REVENUE MODEL: CREATING A SUSTAINABLE AND PROFITABLE BUSINESS

Introduction

The revenue model is a crucial component of your pitch deck, as it outlines how your startup will generate income and sustain profitability. A well-designed revenue model demonstrates to investors that your business is not only innovative but also financially viable. In this chapter, we will explore various revenue models and how to present them effectively to capture the attention of potential investors.

Subscription Model

The subscription model is a popular approach for both B2B and B2C services. It involves offering a recurring service or access to your product in exchange for a regular fee. When presenting this model, highlight the value proposition of your subscription service and the features customers will receive at different price tiers.

Example:

- Freemium Plan: Offer limited features for free to attract users, and entice them to upgrade to premium plans for additional functionalities.
- Premium Plan: Provide full access to all features at a fixed monthly or yearly subscription fee.
- Enterprise Plan: Tailor plans for businesses, offering advanced features, dedicated support, and scalable pricing based on company size.

Product-Based Model

For startups selling physical or digital products, the product-based model centers on pricing and projected sales figures. Present the unique selling points of your product and how it addresses customer needs. Focus on realistic sales projections based on market research and competitive analysis.

Example:

- Product Pricing: Clearly outline the cost of your product and any pricing tiers you may have based on features or quantities.
- Sales Projections: Provide an overview of your projected sales growth over a specific timeframe, taking into account market demand and potential expansion.

Ad Placements and Promotions

If your startup relies on advertising revenue, illustrate how ads will be integrated into your platform and how advertisers will purchase space or promotions. Demonstrate the target audience and how your platform provides value to both users and advertisers.

Example:

- Ad Placement: Show visually where ads will be displayed in your platform or app, demonstrating non-intrusive integration.
- Target Advertisers: Identify potential advertisers and industries that align with your target audience, highlighting the potential for ad revenue growth.

Conclusion

The revenue model is a fundamental aspect of your pitch deck, revealing how your startup will monetize its offerings and achieve financial sustainability.

By presenting a well-defined subscription model with compelling pricing tiers, showcasing realistic sales projections for your product-based model, or highlighting seamless ad placements and potential advertisers, you can instill confidence in investors about the revenue-generating potential of your business.

Remember to align your revenue model with your overall business strategy and target market, ensuring a harmonious pitch that resonates with investors and leads to successful funding opportunities.

CHAPTER 12: UNLOCKING INVESTMENT OPPORTUNITIES: FUNDING YOUR STARTUP'S GROWTH

In the dynamic world of startups, securing investment plays a pivotal role in propelling growth and achieving remarkable success. This chapter embarks on an exploration of the diverse investor landscape, various investment types, funding avenues, and the instrumental role of startup accelerators in the investment quest. Moreover, we delve into strategic approaches for establishing connections with investors, both in the realm of social media and the real world.

Exploring the Investor Spectrum:

Within the vast expanse of investors, startups encounter several categories of funders, including:

Visionary Angel Investors: These individuals pour their personal funds into startups, exchanging capital for an ownership stake.

Venture Capitalists: As seasoned professionals, venture capitalists focus on early-stage startups, injecting funds in exchange for equity.

Crowdfunding Dynamics: Crowdfunding surfaces as a contemporary avenue, collecting smaller contributions from a wide-ranging audience through online platforms.

Strategic Corporate Investors: Large corporations occasionally venture into the startup world, investing in startups either for equity or to forge strategic alliances.

Venturing into Investment Types:

For startups seeking investment, a spectrum of options presents itself:

Seeding the Idea: Pre-seed and seed funding breathe life into a startup, nurturing the initial product or service development.

Scaling Up: Series A, B, and C funding steps in during the later stages, igniting the business's expansion and operational growth.

Harnessing Debt Financing: Debt instruments, such as loans and credit lines, emerge as financial allies to fuel startup expansion.

Mapping the Funding Landscape:

Amidst the labyrinth of funding, startups can chart their course through several funding sources:

- Seeking Support from Familiar Circles: Close-knit connections like friends and family, who genuinely embrace the founder's vision, can turn into reliable funding sources.
- Embracing Angel Networks: Angel groups convene individual investors, synergizing their financial resources to back promising startups.
- Venturing into Venture Capital: Venture capital firms professionally facilitate investment in the early stages of startups.
- Leaning on Crowdfunding Platforms: Online platforms offer startups a digital podium to amass funds from a vast audience.

Navigating the Investor Ecosystem:

In today's interconnected world, establishing connections with potential investors can prove to be a game-changer. Here are strategic methods to traverse the investor ecosystem:

- Handshakes at Networking Events: Local startup gatherings, conferences, and pitch competitions emerge as the perfect grounds to forge real-world connections with potential investors. Armed with a crisp pitch and business cards, entrepreneurs can leave indelible imprints.
- A Social Media Odyssey: In the digital realm, social media stands tall as a powerful tool. Investors are accessible on platforms like LinkedIn and Twitter, where engaging with them, sharing industry insights, and showcasing expertise can foster fruitful relationships.
- Introductions: Nurturing the power of networks, entrepreneurs can seek warm introductions from mutual connections, significantly amplifying the odds of landing meetings with potential investors.
- The Art of Compelling Content: By sharing compelling content, such as blog posts, articles, and videos that illuminate the startup's journey, product, and growth, entrepreneurs can captivate investor attention both online and in relevant communities.

The Crucial Role of Startup Accelerators:

Embarking on a transformative journey, startup accelerators pave the way for early-stage startups by providing essential resources, mentorship, and funding. Usually spanning several months, these programs offer investments in exchange for equity stakes.

The Art of Crafting an Email Pitch:

When approaching investors via email, entrepreneurs must wield the art of crafting compelling and concise messages. Vital tips for a remarkable email pitch include:

- Embrace Brevity: Respect investors' time by keeping emails concise and focused.

- Spotlight the Value Proposition: Clearly articulate how the startup's offering uniquely addresses a problem or fulfills a need.
- Attach Supporting Documents: Supplement the pitch with attachments like pitch decks and financial projections for comprehensive insights.
- Personalize the Message: Tailor each email to the investor's interests and background, showcasing meticulous research.
- A Call to Action: Conclude the email with a clear call to action, inviting further discussions.
- The Gentle Follow-Up: In case of silence, a polite follow-up email acts as a gentle nudge.

A Resilient Journey:

Raising investment unveils itself as an arduous yet rewarding process. Founders must exercise patience, persistence, and an unwavering commitment to their vision. The journey might entail rejections and challenges, but these experiences foster growth, learning, and refinement of approach.

In Conclusion:

Raising investment lays the foundation for a startup's growth trajectory. By comprehending the investor spectrum, understanding investment types, and navigating diverse funding sources, entrepreneurs can unearth opportunities that drive their startup to remarkable heights.
The significance of startup accelerators in the early stages of the journey cannot be overstated, as they provide a nurturing ecosystem for growth. Engaging investors both in the real and virtual world, founders can forge meaningful connections that set the stage for transformative partnerships. As the fundraising quest unfolds, concise and compelling communication shines as the key to success, capturing investor attention and opening doors to prosperity.

CHAPTER 13: THE ART OF CONNECTIONS: UNLEASHING THE POTENTIAL OF NETWORKING IN STARTUP GROWTH

In the journey of building a successful startup, networking plays a pivotal role. It holds the key to establishing meaningful connections with individuals and organizations that can offer invaluable support, guidance, and opportunities for growth. This chapter delves into the profound significance of networking, its myriad benefits, and effective strategies to expand your network, complemented by real-life anecdotes that exemplify its impact on startup achievements.

The Significance of Networking:

Networking brings forth a wealth of advantages for startups, including:

Access to Funding: Forge connections with potential investors to unlock funding opportunities. Consider the story of Dropbox, where founders Drew Houston and Arash Ferdowsi secured essential funding from Y Combinator after meeting one of the program's partners, Paul Graham, at a networking event. This infusion of capital catapulted Dropbox into the successful cloud storage platform it is today.

Industry Insights: Networking provides access to industry experts who can offer invaluable insights and advice. Take Slack, for instance, initially a side project by Stewart Butterfield and his team. Through networking, Butterfield connected with industry insiders, receiving critical feedback that shaped the product's transformation into the widely acclaimed workplace communication tool it is today.

Business Development: Leverage networking to identify potential partners or customers interested in your product or service. Tesla, for example, formed strategic partnerships through networking, such as its collaboration with Panasonic for battery production.

Support and Mentorship: Cultivating a robust network creates a supportive community of peers and mentors who can guide startups through the challenges of establishing a successful business. Airbnb's founders experienced the power of networking when they connected with Y Combinator's Paul Graham, who became a mentor and played a pivotal role in their early success.

Strategies to Expand Your Network:

Master the art of networking by employing these effective strategies:

Attend Industry Events: Actively participate in conferences, trade shows, and industry events to connect with professionals in your field. Such gatherings provide fertile ground for networking and gaining valuable insights into the latest industry trends.

Join Industry Associations: Become a member of relevant industry associations to access like-minded professionals, valuable resources, and events that foster your startup's growth.

Leverage Social Media: Embrace the potential of social media platforms, particularly LinkedIn, to connect with peers, engage in relevant groups, and share updates about your business. Active participation establishes your reputation as an industry expert.

Seek Mentorship: Identify experienced entrepreneurs or industry veterans who can offer guidance, support, and valuable connections to accelerate your startup's journey.

Volunteer: Engage in volunteer work aligned with your values to meet individuals who share similar interests and expand your network. Volunteering also enhances your reputation as a socially responsible entrepreneur.

Participate in Startup Accelerators: Enroll your startup in reputable accelerators like Y Combinator, Techstars, or 500 Startups to gain access to a supportive community of peers and mentors, along with resources and funding that fuel your startup's growth.

In Conclusion:

Networking stands as a cornerstone in the edifice of a successful startup. By expanding your network and nurturing connections with individuals and organizations in your industry, you unlock a treasure trove of invaluable resources, advice, and growth opportunities.

Armed with the strategies outlined in this chapter and inspired by real-world anecdotes, you are well-equipped to expand your network and position your startup for extraordinary success.

CHAPTER 14: BUILDING A LASTING IMPRESSION: CRAFTING A STRONG BRAND

In the dynamic landscape of startups, branding and marketing serve as the bedrock for sustainable growth and success. A robust brand and well-thought-out marketing strategy can differentiate startups from competitors, foster customer trust, and fuel sales. This chapter delves into the essentials of creating a compelling brand and marketing strategy, encompassing the development of a brand identity, defining the target market, crafting a messaging strategy, and executing a comprehensive marketing plan.

Crafting a Compelling Brand Identity:

At the heart of every successful brand lies its identity – a reflection of its values, personality, and vision. Creating a captivating brand identity entails crafting a name, logo, and visual language that resonates deeply with the essence of the brand. Striving for uniqueness and memorability is key, ensuring consistency across all marketing channels, from websites and social media to packaging and products.

Defining the Target Market:

Understanding the ideal customer is paramount in defining the target market. Unveiling demographics, psychographics, and behaviors paints a clear picture of the audience your startup seeks to engage. Conducting in-depth market research identifies pain points, motivations, and desires, facilitating tailored marketing strategies that resonate with the intended audience.

Crafting a Compelling Messaging Strategy:

Once the target market is identified, crafting a messaging strategy that speaks directly to their needs and preferences becomes vital.

A well-honed messaging strategy communicates the brand's unique value proposition, sets it apart from competitors, and establishes a meaningful connection with the target market. Clarity, conciseness, and memorability are the pillars of an impactful messaging strategy.

Executing an Effective Marketing Plan:

Executing the marketing plan translates the strategies into action across various channels. Choosing the right platforms to reach the target market effectively is crucial. Social media, email marketing, content marketing, influencer marketing, public relations, and advertising all play integral roles in a comprehensive marketing approach. Analyzing marketing metrics allows startups to refine their strategies, optimizing channels for maximum impact.

Examples of Successful Branding and Marketing Strategies:

Numerous startups have achieved extraordinary success through robust branding and marketing strategies. For instance, consider Airbnb's strong brand identity, effectively conveying values of community, trust, and belonging. Its messaging strategy emphasizes providing travelers with authentic local experiences, while marketing efforts span social media, content, and influencer collaboration.

Dollar Shave Club stands as another exemplar, challenging traditional razor companies through a unique brand identity. Its messaging strategy centers around offering high-quality razors at an affordable price, supported by a viral marketing campaign and influencer engagement.

In conclusion, branding and marketing are indispensable elements for startup success. A strong brand identity, well-defined target market, compelling messaging strategy, and effective marketing plan are the cornerstones that differentiate startups and inspire customer trust, propelling them toward their business objectives.

By following the strategies outlined in this chapter and studying successful examples of branding and marketing, entrepreneurs can lay a solid foundation for their startups and pave the path to enduring triumph.

Examples:

- Brand Identity: Craft a logo and visual language reflecting eco-friendliness and sustainability, using natural colors to underscore environmental consciousness.
- Target Market: Environmentally conscious individuals, urban gardeners, and those seeking to reduce their ecological footprint.
- Messaging Strategy: Communicate the benefits of biodegradable plant pots, highlighting reduced waste and sustainable gardening practices.
- Marketing Plan: Utilize environmentally conscious social media platforms, share educational content, and collaborate with sustainability influencers.
- Brand Identity: Develop a logo and visuals evoking the outdoors and adventure, employing bright colors to express excitement in discovering new parks.
- Target Market: Families with children, outdoor enthusiasts, and those seeking local adventures.
- Marketing Plan: Leverage social media for user-generated content, collaborate with tourism boards and outdoor organizations.
    EdTechEz:

- Brand Identity: Create a logo and visuals that signify innovation, learning, and technology, with vibrant colors appealing to a broad audience.
- Target Market: Students, educators, and parents seeking innovative educational tools and resources.
- Marketing Plan: Utilize content marketing with valuable educational resources, partner with influencers, and participate in education-focused events.
- Brand Identity: Develop a logo and visuals that convey trust, reliability, and healthcare innovation, using soothing colors for a sense of calm.
- Target Market: Individuals with chronic health conditions, caregivers, and healthcare professionals.
- Messaging Strategy: Focus on the benefits of the MedRmdr device, such as improved medication adherence and better health outcomes.
- Marketing Plan: Engage in targeted social media advertising, collaborate with healthcare influencers, and participate in healthcare events.
- Brand Identity: Create a logo and visuals representing flexibility, productivity, and modern work culture, using a mix of bold and neutral colors.
- Target Market: Remote workers, freelancers, digital nomads, and businesses seeking flexible workspaces.
- Messaging Strategy: Highlight the benefits of using WorknFlx, including access to a network of workspaces and cost savings.
- Marketing Plan: Utilize remote work-focused social media, collaborate with influencers, and partner with coworking spaces and companies.
- Brand Identity: Develop a logo and visuals evoking warmth, love, and companionship, using soft and bright colors for a friendly atmosphere.
- Target Market: Pet lovers, people looking to adopt pets, and animal shelters or rescue centers.
- Messaging Strategy: Emphasize the benefits of using PetndPair to find the perfect pet match with comprehensive matching algorithms and personalized pet recommendations.
- Marketing Plan: Leverage pet lover-focused social media, share heartwarming success stories, collaborate with pet influencers, and participate in pet-related events.

CHAPTER 15: AMPLIFYING GROWTH THROUGH SALES MASTERY

In the dynamic world of startups, sales serve as the heartbeat of success, powering growth and sustainability. In this chapter, we explore the critical components of effective sales, encompassing the formulation of a sales strategy, identification of potential customers, fostering meaningful relationships, and sealing the deal with finesse.

Creating an Impactful Sales Strategy:

At the core of triumphant sales lies a well-crafted strategy that acts as a roadmap to success. This entails outlining sales objectives, defining the target market, and devising strategic sales tactics. A successful sales strategy is rooted in thorough market research, gaining valuable insights into the pain points, motivations, and preferences of the target audience. It should offer a compelling value proposition that sets the startup apart from competitors and resonates deeply with the target market. Additionally, the strategy should incorporate measurable metrics to assess the efficacy of sales endeavors.

Identifying Potential Customers:

Unearthing potential customers involves gaining a profound understanding of the target market and their unique needs. By constructing buyer personas that embody the ideal customer, startups can tailor their sales efforts to align seamlessly with specific requirements and preferences. Market research and data analysis prove indispensable in pinpointing potential customers and deciphering their behavioral patterns. Armed with this knowledge, startups can design an impactful sales strategy that genuinely connects with their intended audience.

Nurturing Enduring Customer Relationships:

Building meaningful relationships with potential customers is a cornerstone of thriving sales efforts. Establishing trust and rapport is essential, entailing active listening to grasp customer needs and preferences fully. By nurturing these relationships over time, startups can cultivate customer loyalty and pave the way for enduring business relationships.

Sealing the Deal with Finesse:

The pinnacle of the sales process involves sealing the deal and converting potential customers into loyal patrons. This entails skillful employment of sales techniques such as negotiation, objection handling, and persuasive tactics. Exuding confidence, clarity, and conciseness in the sales pitch proves pivotal in addressing potential concerns and artfully sealing the deal. By mastering this aspect, startups can successfully generate revenue and foster a dedicated customer base.

CHAPTER 16: THE ENGINE OF GROWTH: NURTURING EFFICIENT OPERATIONS FOR STARTUP SUCCESS

A thriving startup's success hinges on its ability to manage operations with finesse. Streamlining processes and optimizing resources are paramount to reduce costs, drive revenue, and foster sustainable growth. This chapter delves into the critical facets of operations management, encompassing supply chain optimization, inventory efficiency, streamlined production, and effective distribution.

Fine-Tuning the Supply Chain:

Efficiently managing the supply chain is the linchpin of a smooth flow of goods and services from suppliers to customers. This involves sourcing reliable suppliers, negotiating contracts, and ensuring seamless logistics for deliveries. An effective supply chain is instrumental in curbing expenses and ensuring timely deliveries.

An exemplary instance of supply chain management can be seen in "vendor-managed inventory" (VMI) by Walmart. By collaborating closely with suppliers, Walmart proficiently monitors inventory levels, restocks products, and ensures prompt delivery. The VMI system has empowered Walmart to cut inventory expenses, mitigate stockouts, and elevate customer satisfaction.

Perfecting Inventory Efficiency:

Inventive inventory management is pivotal in maintaining optimal stock levels, placing strategic orders, and meticulous inventory tracking. A well-honed inventory system is imperative to trim costs and avert stockouts. Employing inventory management systems allows real-time monitoring, data-driven adjustments, and enhanced efficiency aligned with customer demand.

Amazon's successful adoption of the "Just-in-Time" (JIT) inventory system illustrates excellent inventory management. By leveraging JIT to minimize inventory costs and enhance efficiency, Amazon orders products solely upon customer purchases, sidestepping excess inventory and reducing stockout risks.

Enhancing Production Processes:

Exemplary production management involves overseeing production processes, resources, and equipment to minimize costs and elevate efficiency. A streamlined production process is vital for on-time product delivery and cost optimization.

Toyota's acclaimed "lean production" system exemplifies a successful production management strategy. This system revolves around waste reduction, optimizing production processes, and continuously improving efficiency. Embracing lean production has empowered Toyota to achieve cost savings, enhance product quality, and reduce lead times.

Streamlining Distribution Channels:

Effective distribution management entails handling logistics to deliver goods and services promptly to customers. This process entails optimizing distribution channels to ensure efficient product delivery while reducing costs. Effective distribution management fosters heightened customer satisfaction and cost-effectiveness.

FedEx's well-organized logistics network is a case in point of successful distribution management. The network prioritizes optimized delivery routes, advanced tracking technology, and exceptional customer service. FedEx's logistics network has culminated in cost savings, improved delivery times, and enhanced customer satisfaction.

In conclusion, efficient operations management serves as the backbone of a successful startup. By optimizing the supply chain, perfecting inventory efficiency, enhancing production processes, and streamlining distribution, entrepreneurs can curtail costs, amplify efficiency, and maximize revenue. Emulating successful operations management strategies and integrating best practices equips startup founders to lay a robust foundation for their venture and accomplish their business objectives.

CHAPTER 17: UNDERSTANDING THE LAW: A COMPREHENSIVE GUIDE TO LEGAL FACTORS IN ENTREPRENEURSHIP

When embarking on the entrepreneurial journey, understanding the legal implications is of utmost importance. The legal panorama of entrepreneurship may seem complicated, but its understanding is critical for your startup to function within the confines of the law and reduce potential legal risks. This chapter elucidates key legal aspects that all entrepreneurs should consider, including protection of intellectual property, determining the business structure, employment regulations, and contract negotiations.

The concept of Intellectual Property (IP) holds great significance for startups. It is essential to shield your IP to deter others from duplicating or capitalizing on your unique ideas, inventions, or brand elements. Familiarizing yourself with different types of IP, such as trademarks, patents, copyrights, and trade secrets, can enable you to employ effective protection strategies.

Choosing the right business structure is pivotal for efficient operation of your startup. It helps mitigate legal risks and optimize tax benefits. Familiarizing yourself with different types of business structures, like sole proprietorship, partnership, Limited Liability Company (LLC), and corporations, can help you understand the differences in liability, ownership, and taxation for each.

Employment law is an essential aspect for startups hiring employees. It involves understanding the legal obligations related to hiring, terminating, and managing employees, including wage and hour laws, discrimination laws, and workers' compensation laws. Compliance with employment laws helps to avoid legal issues and fosters a positive work environment.

Contracts are fundamental for businesses involved in transactions with suppliers, customers, or partners. Understanding various types of contracts, such as sales contracts, lease agreements, and licensing agreements, and effective negotiation and enforcement of these contracts, is crucial for smooth business operations.

In conclusion, legal considerations are an integral part of entrepreneurship. By thoroughly understanding the legal aspects and forming efficient legal strategies, entrepreneurs can safeguard their assets, lessen legal risks, and maximize success potential. Therefore, a robust legal foundation is a key to achieving business objectives.